All of my life I have worked with computers in design, marketing and sales, with corporate companies, such as Canon and Motorola, both in the UK and abroad.

I have been trained in problem solving at a residential course at Oxford College, and also attended several courses in Sales and Marketing, by IBM.

Over my time I have been the top sales person within the companies that I have worked with, in using the problem techniques I have outlined in this book. So this book will introduce you in how to use all of the outstanding techniques and ideas to overcome any problem that you may face, with easy to use complex solutions.

Being suitable for any individual, company or cooperate business this book will be highly beneficial for anybody who wants to improve their lifestyle and achieve success in everything that they wish to master.

Martin Harvey

PROBLEM SOLVING FOR INDIVIDUALS AND COMPANIES

AUSTIN MACAULEY PUBLISHERS™

LONDON · CAMBRIDGE · NEW YORK · SHARJAH

A CIP catalogue record for this title is available from the British Library.

ISBN 9781398472044 (Paperback)
ISBN 9781398472068 (ePub e-book)

www.austinmacauley.com

First Published 2022
Austin Macauley Publishers Ltd®
1 Canada Square
Canary Wharf
London
E14 5AA

Table of Contents

Preview

Every person has problems to solve whether they are large or small. This is also true about companies as well.

This book will provide all of the different solutions that you require, covering all of the problem-solving techniques that have been used together with lots of new ideas that will assist you now and in the future. It also teaches you how to be more productive and successful in your lifestyle. This includes personal problems, relationships, health and wellbeing.

In addition, it also guides you on how to run a business that provides you with greater achievement, faster growth and financial security.

How to Negotiate Anything

The whole world is a giant negotiating emporium and, whether you like it or not, you will come into conflict with family members, other individuals, companies, or competitors at some time. How you handle these encounters can determine not only whether you prosper, but also that you should be able to enjoy a full and satisfying life. Your ability to negotiate determines whether you can or cannot influence your environment. If you can, then this gives you a sense of mastery over your life.

Basically, it comes down to analysing everything around you including understanding the situation alongside your own personal experiences.

So negotiating is the use of information, timing and power to affect the behaviour within a web of tension and used intelligently to reach your goal. In achieving this, it is important that you obtain the co-operation, help and support of different people to build an important informative structure to assist you on the way forward to success.

There are three things that are absolutely vital in successful negotiation:

- Information

To start with, the first thing you need is correct and accurate information before the meeting takes place or when the negotiation begins.

First find out about the individual as much as you can, including discussions with his friends and contacts. Be honest with everyone as this will assist you in the negotiation stage as well as the final outcome. Information can be thought of as the resolution of uncertainty, as it answers the question of what an entity is and thus defines both its essence, meanings, and the nature of its characteristics. So therefore, information is used for understanding the situation which then becomes knowledge.

- Timing

The second thing that is extremely important is timing. If you have requested the relevant information and the client is not sure about the timing prospects, then ask him about previous similar projects that he is familiar with. This should then throw more information about the similar timing aspects. Sometimes the other side does not seem to be under the same kind of organisational pressure that you are feeling. So just ask the question is the matter to be finalised on the day of discussion or will it be delayed within a given timescale that fits within the project requirement.

Understandably, timing is the choice of judgement or the control of something when it happens. This should then provide you with the ability to control the outcome at exactly the right time. The way we view and use time can be crucial to achieving success. Timing is just as important as information because putting these two components together gives you the power to control the negotiation. So, this will assist you in helping to understand the true picture that is happening before you.

- Gaining power

Power is a mind-blowing entity as it provides the capacity and ability to get things done. In addition to this it also exercises control over people, events, situations, and oneself. However, all power is based on perception. But this can be improved if you think that you have it, combined with the information and timing to enhance your opportunity of arriving at a successful conclusion. Your ability to negotiate determines whether you can influence your environment. This gives you a sense of mastery over your life and others. So, analysing all of the information and timing will give you the power to affect the behaviour in the negotiation to make things happen the way you want them to.

Achieving Mutual Satisfaction

If you have a problem, then it is important to switch the relationship from a competitive win/lose contest to a collaborative encounter in which you can both meet your needs. A negotiation is more than an exchange of material objects. It is a way of acting and behaving that can develop understanding, belief, acceptance respect and trust. It is the manner of your approach, the tone of your voice, the attitude that you convey and the methods you use as well as the concern that you exhibit in understanding the other side's feelings and needs.

Pursue Alternative Paths

Start by challenging the definition of the requirements and expand this opportunity into other solutions that should be considered. The more solutions that you develop should provide you with the correct alternative. Quite often, what appears to be a problem is actually an opportunity in disguise, that has been missed out from the original idea or discussion.

Sometimes the quality of the solution seems to be in the direct proportion to the quantity of solutions that have been considered. The more possible solutions that you develop assists you to make it more likely that you will come up with the correct overall conclusion.

Weakness

Sometimes weakness can be to your advantage. Either requesting further information or saying, "I am not quite sure about what you have told me." This strategy opens up a level of communication that should provide you with additional information that could be vital to the outcome.

Combat Losing

If you feel that you are losing the negotiation within your advantage, then go back with the overall details that you have discussed and ask the question about the information you have provided so far. Then ask where your proposal does not meet with their requirements. This will not only open up a further discussion, giving you an opportunity of having details of where disagreements occur, but it will also provide you with further information for discussion, enabling you to negotiate a better proposal in your favour.

Gaining Control

If it looks as if you are going to lose the agreement between both parties, put all of your cards on the table, including all the information you have, then ask what you have to do to get this agreement or contract finalised. By this time, you should have the negotiating skills within your capability to turn it into a successful conclusion that is acceptable to both parties. If it does not work out in your favour then leave your proposal in case the other party changes his mind or things are not working out with the other offer to his requirements. Always leave the door open. Hopefully this should provide you with a successful outcome.

The Art of Influencing People

Persuasion Skills

Persuasion skills are extremely important as they help individuals to change pre-conceived notions and ideas of potential customers or clients, making them believe what you are telling them. First and foremost is to convince your potential client that you look confident and also have all of the information that he needs about your ideas. So persuasion is many different terms of influence, covering the person's beliefs, attitudes, intentions, motivations and behaviours. This is normally a process aimed at changing a person's attitude or behaviour towards some event, idea, object or other persons by using written or spoken words, or visual tools to convey information, feelings or combination thereof.

These elements are largely emotional, which includes being reliable and taking responsibility, in being sincere, genuine and honest, knowing your subject and believing in it, by building rapport and being entertaining, as well as not arguing but providing solutions that work on a mutual basis. So, the key to successful persuasion includes having self-esteem and good emotional intelligence. They also believe that they will succeed and remain motivated in having to believe in yourself as well as in your ideas.

Gifts

People are more pleased and thankful when they receive an unexpected present that they like or can see the enjoyment it will bring. Everyone loves presents, particularly when they are free.

After they have received the gift, they will then feel obliged to return the favour of the gift. This will make them feel satisfied about the transaction. When this happens, both of you will have enhanced your relationship, which means that you have built a stronger rapport in creating a far better understanding of each other.

Praise and Appreciation

Praise is one of the most powerful things anyone can offer when delivered well and it is deserved. It gives people the drive and motivation to continue achieving the calibre of work which both of you want to see.

A simple "thank you" can make a big difference to them, or some personal recognition of them can make all the difference. If you are trying to catch up on someone's weakness, praise can make all the difference. It takes hard work and focus to improve at something you are struggling with. Giving them purpose and thoughtful gifts as well as giving praise is a major boost of confidence and it will be appreciated. But it needs to be sincere as, at the same time, it is a skill that is highly accepted, however it does take time to develop. Finally, giving not enough praise can make people demoralised, whereas too much praise can sometimes make others start questioning your motives.

Body Language

Body language is the show part of being confident about yourself, which reveals our true feelings and emotions that other people will respect. So, if you appear more positive, engaging, and approachable, this will make others feel more assured about you.

Names of People

Smiling, knowing someone's name and praising people, as well as making the effort to know their interests and talking to them makes people feel important. Remembering someone's name makes them feel special and important enough to open up other discussions, with them doing most of the talking. This enables you to understand the individual much better and what his expectations are, which enhances building a special relationship between both of you, as this can work exponentially in providing more pleasant experiences of life together.

Interest in Other People – Important Criteria

- Use your influence and charisma at all times.
- Before you try to influence someone, create a relationship with them without asking for something in return.
- Pay attention to your body language, and theirs, as this can give away your confidence level without saying anything.

- Convince the person you are talking to that what you are suggesting is the easiest and the fastest solution for their problem.
- When people know what to expect, they create expectations which can be enhanced to make the final decision.
- There is no better way of understanding people than putting yourself in their shoes. This allows you to understand their opinion from within their perspective.
- If you understand that you are getting close to the final goal and making the solution offer, then you are ready to use your power of persuasion to achieve the outcome in your favour.

So, all of the above principles can make people feel more important, including most other people that look up to authority within any field or subject. Hence this makes you seem as a source of authority that can take you a long way towards an agreement.

Growing Your Company – Cost Effectively

So basically, you are asking your existing customer base if they can think of 2 potential companies that could benefit from the services that you offer.

This can then produce at least one referral per customer to enhance your customer base. Then, obviously, contact your new customers to see if they know of anybody that could be interested in your company's products or services.

This system can also work in your favour if you ask all of your friends if they know of anybody who might have a requirement for what you are offering. Amazingly enough, this continued referral system has obvious advantages over and above any other system of finding new customers without any finance being involved.

There are techniques or suitable methods in growing the size of your company by using minimal finance requirements. First of all, you need to analyse the structure of your company in the following way: List all the major customers that you currently have, listing their size and what business they are in. Then list all of the other companies that you are not doing business with and compare the balance between your existing customers and new potentials. Call the potential companies and talk to their marketing department, their purchasing management team and production people and ask them if they would like to do business with you, after explaining what you offer in the way of products, manufacturing, and support services. This is the most cost-effective method in finding new business which relates to the existing customer base.

Charm Delivers

The word charm originates from the Latin – "carmen", which means "song".

Charm is one of the wonders of the world, as it is described as the power or quality of delighting, attracting as well as fascinating other people. It is also an object or saying that is thought to have special or magical powers to draw in another person by exerting a powerful influence over them. It combines the power of pleasing or attracting something through personality or beauty. The different types of charm mostly relate to attraction, pleasing someone, or good luck. People that have magnetic personalities make you want to hang out with them, as they are pleasing enough to allow someone to be attracted to them and allow them to win them over. Charming people are confident enough to show a little vulnerability. They know that, while some people are temporarily impressed by what is artificial, everyone sincerely likes and appreciates the genuine details and the conclusion.

If someone has charm, they always show that they are genuinely pleased to meet you. This then creates a bond between both parties, which builds an understanding withing a given level of confidence. This enables charming people to always search for agreement because exchanging opinions and ideas, as well as treating everyone in the same way, is very deserving of respect and kindness.

Posture

Proper posture is very important in impressing someone that you might not know, as it enhances confidence and provides a charismatic atmosphere to all others around you. Sometimes when you are sure about having a physical contact with someone, just a hand on a shoulder or perhaps a hug can produce amazing results of reassurance within anybody that you meet. They will feel the charm within you. Which can make both of you more relaxed and feel closer together in harnessing the interchange of energy which both of you will benefit from.

Finally, your confidence will spill over to other people who are impressed with your charming capability, in which they wish to learn from you and implement within their lifestyle the exact same charm, charisma and character that you have yourself.

Remember: It is nice to be important, but it is more important to be nice.

The Benefits of Teamwork

Teamwork is not only vital but is essential within any company or organisation to bring a relationship of minds and things together, which can show an important increase of collaboration. Working together can achieve a lot more of both efficiency and effectiveness towards reaching a common goal of achievements. The enhancements of co-workers with proven diverse experience, skills, work, and histories can provide a fertile ground for brain-storming and creative problem solving. When you have more than one person involved in a complex environment then this brings together more enthusiasm and complementary skills which enables you to expand into a far greater sense of direction. So, it becomes synergistic that when several people are together it means that they are more powerful when they work together instead of being on their own. There is also more enthusiasm in building up collaboration, in working efficiently and effectively within a team in sharing experiences and learning from each other.

Trust

Trust also naturally develops when team members rely on each other combined with strengthened working relationships which creates an environment so that employees can open up about concerns and offering new ideas that can encourage each other to advance in communicating at different levels with each other.

When you look at each of the employees, they all have different skill sets, but this is one of the benefits when you gather them all together. So, working with each other can strengthen your teams efforts in making them more effective than working alone.

The importance of teamwork is the fostering of healthy conflict producing resolution skills. Even team members from time to time may disagree on occasions, but a strong team will listen to each other's concerns and work together towards a mutually agreeable solution.

Teams Attract Talent

It is difficult to remain unengaged when your teammates are excited about an important project that affects everyone involved. As enthusiasm grows within a team then this will attract other individuals to join in, which can enhance the project outcome.

Teamwork Benefits

1) Working synergistically, improves performance and can work out how to solve problems providing a better sense of direction with the right results.
2) Trust is an important building block that naturally occurs when team members are all working and relying on each other while working for results.

3) Working in collaboration builds exciting projects as co-workers feeding off others enthusiasm improving important projects that affect everyone.

4) The importance of teamwork members are attracted to companies that build teamwork into their corporate cultures and will also be attracting new talent in the future.

5) Employees who work alone can be concerned about taking risks on their own, so this can prevent them from sharing potentially new ground-breaking ideas. However, working towards a shared goal increases internal communication which provides a safe space in which out of the box thinking promotes better results.

There is also better judgement in analysing the information that is available to you, that improves strategy when there is more than one decision maker. It is also easier to take control of the situation where there is mutual consistency amongst all of the individuals.

The Benefits of Trust

Trust is feeling that somebody or something can be relied upon, or the outcome will turn out to be good. It is also feeling sure about something even if it cannot be proved. The four elements of trust are consistency, compassion, communication, and competency. So, you will find that trust is difficult to achieve, btu impossible to ignore. Trust is also one of the most important features of our lives. It takes a long time to build up trust with an individual, families, companies, or business colleagues including politics, but it can be lost or destroyed within a very short space of time. Therefore, every effort must be deployed to keep all of the trust levels that you have within your control.

Trust can easily be lost suddenly by just saying the wrong thing or doing something that is unacceptable. So, regaining lost trust is a very difficult thing to achieve and can last a long time that feels like forever. Sometimes apologies do not always work in your favour, even if they are offered in a sincere way, so you may not always win your own way. As time goes by, the best approach would be to assist this person with supportive help when they have a problem or a setback in life. This should be well accepted and can lead to regaining their trust.

Companies

Unfortunately, once you have lost trust with your customer then this is the slippery slope of possibly losing turnover, profit and long-term customers, which can end up in an uncontrollable disaster. So, exercise overall control in keeping your trust levels with your existing customers as well as using this platform covering the future trust within your organisation together with an ongoing commitment to all customers.

If this does not work, then try to get yourself in a better situation which would call for thinking more deeply about the situation before saying something or holding back on doing anything which could upset anyone after the event. So, it would be better to think of the consequences more than once and then try to work out what is going to be the best possible result.

It is also more catastrophic when companies completely lose the trust of their customers. This has occurred may times with banks when their IT systems stop working for a period of time and existing customers cannot access their money. 42%of banks over the last year (2020) have had IT problems which affected their customers on a grand scale and puts pressure on existing staff who have to liaise with highly annoyed individuals. So, this requires better IT tested security systems in providing the security required to enable your company not to be open to any cyber-attacks.

Consent

Overall consent must be freely given to individuals and companies, as this means you are giving people genuine ongoing choices and control over how you use their data. It should be obvious and require a positive action to opt in. So, requests must be prominent and unbundled from other terms and conditions. It also must be easy to understand and user-friendly.

Remember: Trust can take years to build, seconds to break and forever to repair.

The Ingenuity of Einstein

Working through a conflict or situation, Einstein used a powerful visual image of the problem regarding how things work. Sometimes he would use a brick-by-brick process, slowly putting together a complete image of what he was thinking. This encouraged him to study technical details of new designs at a fast speed of light through visualisation using the thought of a new experiment.

Mind Power

Mind power is fascinating, so take time to read and explore how your thoughts and actions can essentially change your life using crucial information in focussing your thoughts and beliefs in order to change everything for the better.

Statement

Einstein also said that imagination is everything. It is the preview of life's coming attractions.

Einstein's Quotations

Being Right

"I think and think for months and years. Ninety-nine times the conclusion is false. The hundredth time I am right."

New Thoughts

"To raise new questions, new possibilities, to regard old problems from a new angle, requires creative imagination and that marks real advance in science."

Information

"Information is not knowledge, but it can be more important than knowledge."

Imagination

"However imagination embraces the entire world, its stimulating progress gives birth to evolution."

Thinking

"We can't solve problems by using the same kind of thinking we used when we first created them."

Words

"I rarely think in words at all. A thought comes and I may try to express it in words afterwards."

His Thought Process

Einstein went about his work in unique ways, from visualisation to daydreaming and even using a musical inspiration, which enabled him to have creative insights and philosophical vantage points which can still help the work we tackle today. He not only took breaks to play the violin, but he also took long vigorous walks on which he carried a pencil and a blank sheet of paper wo write ideas down. May other creative and successful people believed in the power of the regular, scheduled midday walk, including Tchaikovsky.

As part of their creative process this was to adapt to combinatory play, which takes unrelated things outside the realm of science, including art, ideas, music and thoughts as well as blending them together to come up with new ideas.

Big Problems Solved

We have all suffered from big problems that get in the way of achieving our ambitions and desires in life. A good start is breaking down the gap between the problem and the solution into smaller milestones and achieving smaller goals. It is worth setting this down on paper to identify how big the gap is and how many milestones there are between the two. This helps the brain to absorb the information on the page and this starts the analytical part of the brain to engage in looking at the entire problem as well as thinking about achieving the individual milestones. These milestones guide everyone towards achieving their dreams, which keeps them motivated to carry on finding the solution. To start with it does not matter which milestone you choose. Once you have laid out your achievement plan, then figure out the most effective way to achieve each smaller goal and write down the actions that are needed. Then form a hypothesis about how to close the gap by listing as may options and ideas as possible by analysing and developing an action plan. Even if you stumble at one of the milestones, move on to the next one, which will help clear your mind for the new information and a possible solution. It is worth going up and down the milestone level several times, adding to the information that you already have written down.

If you have had enough of approaching this style, give it a break and come back tomorrow with a clear set of targets to start on. If possible, outline some of the more difficult milestone levels with friends or colleagues to gain further ideas to reconsider the problem.

To achieve the most impact with good results, you need to have an effective plan and great execution. If you have one, but not the other, then you will not be able to reach your goal. You need both as they work synergistically together in achieving the best results. This plan should give you an excellent opportunity, enabling you to achieve a very effective conclusion in the way to implement and execute your way to success.

Finally, do not forget to write a concrete schedule, by writing down everything that you are going to do and when you are going to do it. It also helps to monitor your progress and revise your plan as necessary.

Size Matters

Size is everything, whether in your lifestyle or business. As it can grow or diminish at any time without you realising it.

Let's look at business to start with, such as why many large retail businesses have gone out of business. The reason for this is that as these businesses have grown in the past, they have not looked at or understood the business model as it changes and the impact this has on the turnover and profit of any business. The important thing about any company is that you should be in control of the majority of your assets combined with profit margins. For example, if you continue to grow the business by selling the property you own and leasing it back, then you do not own a major part of the assets and you start to lose control. If you continue on this basis, including borrowing money for an expansion programme of the company, then you start to lose control, as the majority of the company turnover is not within your overall control. If this happens, then you start to have a large uncontrollable finance profile, which can be detrimental to the company's financial situation, whereby the lease costs go up out of your control and the payback on the extra loan for expansion can change at any time without you having any influence.

If you own the commercial property, then you have options, such as selling an out-of-town location to a developer for house building, warehouse, or flats to let. This would enable you to relocate to a smaller site, or sites, within a growing potential area that can enhance your sales growth with you still being in control.

Size is more important than you think. Whether this is looked at from an individual, group or company perspective, size should be analysed carefully before you venture into an expansion programme or are developing a reduction of size. Size is not only important, but vital for survival and you have to track the details of this on a regular basis just to stay ahead of the game.

So, take the fiasco of Sainsbury's merging with ASDA. If this merger went ahead, both companies would be making the wrong decision. Basically, this comes down to size, and just because you are a large conglomerate does not mean you are going to improve your profit margin and keep your combined customer base happy. In fact, the reverse would be the true outcome. First of all, after the merger, they were expecting a drop of 10% on the purchase price from their suppliers. This is a fallacy because a lot of their suppliers are currently only making 10% profit margin to begin with, so they are living in cloud cuckoo land. Secondly, they did not take into account the cost and involvement in integrating the two.

Finally, they admitted that if the merger did go ahead then they would have to close several stores where there would be too many joint stores within a certain location. Obviously, this would have a detrimental effect on their sales figures and upset many customers if their local retail outlet closed. Over the last year (2020), Sainsbury's share price has gone down by 12%.

British Airways is another situation. This time buying up other airline companies too quickly and then trying to integrate they data computer systems without having the experience to handle the takeover. In the last year they had the experience of having three glitches in their computer system, which has had catastrophic consequences. They used to be the world's favourite airline, now most of their customers call them just a cheap airline company. Over the last year (2020), IAG shares are down by 9%.

So, this proves that size is very important, whether you are buying up other companies or downsizing. All of the potential problems that may occur would need to be analysed carefully to ensure it does not upset the company's stability or profit margin in the process and in the future.

Super Sales Techniques

The most important thing in sales techniques is to be in control of the situation. This is base around negotiating key elements within the discussion. To achieve this, you need both information and timing. Putting these two vital elements together gives you the power to succeed.

If you do not have one of these elements, then you could fail in your negotiation. Power is a mind-blowing entity, giving you the capacity and ability to get things done and get things that you want. It also involves perception, which is analysing information ant timing, which give you the power to affect behaviour in the meeting of needs to make things happen the way you want them to. Do not be too quick to prove your intellect at the outset of the meeting, as asking questions, even when you think you know the answer, can be quite revealing.

The fact is that you negotiate all the time, both within your occupation and within your personal life. So, you need strong negotiating skills to obtain other people's help and support to make sure that they are on your side.

Important Strategies

1) Talking to all levels within an organisation is vital for successful results. Let everyone know what you are doing and explain what your company offers, especially including the Finance Director, as he will be signing off these transactions.

2) Always ask for referrals at every visit, as this can provide you with important contacts and details of a lead. This can then allow you to follow up on the decision process and allows you to improve on your sales level.

3) When setting up a meeting, always ask everyone to provide their name and business card in front of them, which allows you to remember their name, then ask them briefly what they expect to happen by the end of the meeting.

4) Get to know everyone within each of your customers, including the manufacturing manager. Make a request for you to be shown around their manufacturing/assembly plant, as this might show up component parts that you are not currently supplying them. This then gives you the opportunity to supply more components so as to enhance…

5) Look at the company report to enhance your understanding of the markets that they cover as well as their financial information.

6) Be ready, at any time, to give a presentation about your company to an individual, management, and a board of directors, of what your company can offer, including all products and services.

7) Mention who the customers are that you supply to, as this can give them confidence in dealing with you.

8) Create a company comparison list of similar products and services that you supply, then analyse the larger companies and work out if you can move into this marketplace to create more sales.

9) Always tell the truth as this will help you to gain credibility. Do not tell jokes, instead, tell them an interesting story that will amuse them.

10) When you are negotiating a big deal and you would like it to play more in your favour, make a request to the purchasing manager for permission to write to the board of directors. This will outline what your offer is, together with more useful information about your company. This should put you in a better position, not only to win this particular order, but also to give you more requests about what your company supplies.

11) Always be friendly to secretaries and ask how they are, as they have access to lots of information about their company that can be informative if you ask the right questions.

In any negotiation, you should have control of power by analysing the total situation, regarding the other side's position as well as your own, in order to achieve the outcome you desire. Within reason, you should always get whatever you want, providing that you are aware of your options. If you test your assumptions and take shrewdly calculated risks, that are based on solid information and timing requirements, then you should have the power to succeed. If you have the power, then you will be conveying the self-confidence of perception, which will enable others to believe in you. This enables you to achieve the desired result within a negotiated environment.

Remember: Telling the truth gives you the power that nobody else can challenge.

Diversity

Diversity in the workplace is important, but quite often it is forgotten about. Utilising a diverse workforce can lead to greater motivation amongst staff, as well as producing more innovative ideas in finding solutions to existing problems. When companies commit themselves to diverse leadership, then they become more successful.

The companies using this technique invariably have the opportunity to employ the top talented people as well as improving customer service, employee satisfaction, including the decision-making process. This all leads to improvement in financial returns. For example, both ethnic and gender diversity can enhance the profit of a company by 15% +. This implies that diversity is a competitive element in moving market share more towards the diverse companies. One way in particular as to how this works is that it provides a much better communication level between management and their employees. This then enables the management to consider more options from everyone within your organisation, which provides them with more ideas for improvement in all ways possible. Hence this allows management to make far better decisions which will enhance their capability in problem solving.

Suggestion Box

Some while ago, it was standard practice to attach to the wall a suggestion box that enabled any employee to write down and make a note or a suggestion to improve a situation, or an idea to improve productivity, or just comment about what they thought about the company's forward strategy.

This system worked well for both employees and management in providing much better communication and understanding for all those concerned.

Sometimes management would implement a scheme of creating an employee of the month award, or based on how good their idea was, would result in a financial benefit.

I believe that all companies can benefit both in growth and financially in providing this zero-cost implementation scheme. It is so cost effective in looking at employee comments for improvement as they are working very close to the job required and can easily see opportunities which other people cannot identify with. For example, it would be far more cost effective than bringing in a consultant to survey the same problem. It also keeps everyone focused on the job in hand as well as allowing further understanding of how the company wishes to expand including bringing in better financial results.

So, we know intuitively that diversity matters, as it becomes increasingly clear that it makes pure sense in business terms. Research finds that companies within the top quarter for gender or racial and ethnic diversity are more likely to have financial returns above their national industry standards. And diversity being a competitive differentiator will shift even more market share towards the more diverse companies over time. Finally, diversity is not a problem that needs to be solved. In fact, it is something that should be celebrated, which can add richness, insight, and perspective to every business.

Amazing Astrology

Ancients have been interested in astrology for over 10,000 years, so this makes it the oldest form of divination in the world. Early astrologers noted that most groups of stars, known as constellations, moved around the sky together. They also noticed that the movements of the sun and moon played significantly into understanding the basics of astrology. Then they came to realise that people born at a particular time of year when the sun, moon and planets were in the same part of the sky, had a great deal in common. This enabled astrologers to construct horoscope charts for individual people.

They first of all believed that the building blocks of the universe, such as fire, earth, air and water were the elements that expressed the indispensable nature of the different signs. There are twelve different sections in the sky, each one representing one of the signs of the zodiac. They are as follows:-

Fire Signs: Aries, Leo, and Sagittarius

Fire is positive, assertive, energetic, enthusiastic, impulsive, inspirational, courageous, powerful, passionate, and initiating.

Earth Signs: Taurus, Virgo, and Capricorn

Earth is cautious, responsible, reliable, ambitious, practical, focused, disciplined, dependable, solid, and persevering.

Water Signs: Cancer, Scorpio, and Pisces

Water is compassionate, forgiving, understanding, emotional, creative, intuitive, and spiritual.

Air Signs: Gemini, Libra, and Aquarius

Air is light-hearted, joyful, curious, restless, independent, communicative, impractical, entertaining, intellectual and trusting.

The astrologers refer to ten planets when they are doing their calculations because this assists them when looking at a horoscope chart for understanding astrology in general. This is important as they all have a strong influence on our lives, according to the basics of understanding each of the planets which relates to a different side of our personality.

The Ten Planets

The Sun:

It reveals what we want out of life. The sun is a giver of life, radiating energy, inspiration, self-awareness, enthusiasm, and wisdom. This also relates to the conscious mind.

The Moon

The moon symbolises fertility and relates to sensitivity, imagination, feelings, emotions, the subconscious, and intuition. It also provides nurturing, domesticity, home, and family life.

Mercury

This governs the nervous system and intellect. It relates to self-expression and getting on with others, with the key aspect of communication relating to rapid thought, adaptability, eloquence, and quick perceptions.

Venus

Venus is the goddess of love and sexuality. It represents gentility, sociability, beauty, and the arts. It also controls the deeper human emotions such as appreciation, love, and devotion.

Mars

The god of war symbolises courage, force, bravery, assertiveness, and physical drive. It also gives the qualities of boldness, frankness, endurance, and initiative, revealing your energy and sexuality. It also gives strength of character with a strong will to succeed.

Jupiter

Jupiter is second only to the sun, symbolising wisdom, moderation, generosity, bringing good fortune and luck. It is also related to wisdom, knowledge, learning, philosophy, ethics, and intellect.

Saturn

This is the planet of restriction and restraint. It reveals our sense of discipline, responsibility, focus and strength of character. Providing tenacity, prudence, self-control, and concentration, it can be a positive energy helping people to attain their aims in life.

Uranus

Providing transformation and regeneration, it provides new ideas and concepts, bringing out people's highest potential. It reveals originality, individuality, and creativity, engaging in a humanitarian outlook within a metaphysical pursuit.

Neptune

This rules our innermost feelings, psychic abilities, sensitivity, and imagination. Its main positive traits are perceptiveness, intuition, spiritual development, compassion with humanitarian ideals.

Pluto

This is the ruler of the underworld, representing the subconscious. It also reveals your capacity for change, regeneration, growth, healing, and knowledge. A it takes Pluto 250 years to circle the zodiac, it has an influential effect on generations of people that can also influence world affairs and conditions.

Star Signs

Aries	Mar 21 – April 20
Taurus	April 21 – May 21
Gemini	May 22 – June 22
Cancer	June 23 – July 23
Leo	July 24 – August 23
Virgo	August 24 – September 23
Libra	September 24 – October 23
Scorpio	October 24 – November 22
Sagittarius	November 23 – December 21
Capricorn	December 22 – January 20
Aquarius	January 21 – February 19
Pisces	February 20 – March 20

The aspects of the planets emphasise the positive, beneficial energies indicating the area of life that you can succeed in and what you set out to accomplish with little effort required.

With this information, it is possible to provide a detailed description of the person's personality, including his or her strengths and weaknesses, emotions, parental influence, plus the ability to find happiness and fulfilment, lifestyle and career including love and sex. In fact, using these astrology basics, it is possible to look at a chart and receive information about any aspect of the person's personality and general makeup.

So, astrology doesn't claim to accurately predict the future but, using a variety of methods, it can reveal the influences and tendencies for today. Plus, the possibility of things that are likely to happen in the future, including the dangers to be aware of ahead of you.

So, Star constellations are just as vital to our everyday lives as our smartphones. Just as there are many horoscopes available in both newspapers and supplements for detailed daily information, the following apps available will give you further detailed data regarding personalised astrological charts to assist in predicting daily/monthly horoscope details.

The Best Astrology Apps Available

1) Astrology and palmistry coach

This app gives you daily, monthly and yearly insights into you career, relationships, family and friendships. In addition, it provides you with compatibility reports, numerology, and palm reading. Free from the App Store.

2) Apple.com/us/app/iluna

Iluna is an interactive astrological calendar that allows you to easily find out the lunar phase, the moon's position in the signs of the zodiac. It also provides a description for each phase, sign and mansion. You can navigate through the information in various ways. i.e. on a day-by-day basis.

3) Co-star (costarastrology.com)

This is powered by NASA data and is based on the time, date, and place that you were born. This generates personalised astrological charts to help predict daily horoscopes free of charge.

4) Sanctuary

Provides news and daily horoscopes with live on-demand birth chart readings from professional astrologers. Available from App Store and Google Play Free of charge.

Astrology can give you everything you need to upgrade your life, your happiness, health, and prosperity, including consciousness as well as unlocking the infinite power of your heart and mind every day.

This provides harmony, lasting peace of mind and the flow of energy in every area of your life. It also provides radiant, lifelong health and happiness. So, start living a life of infinite possibility and a conscious lifestyle, joy and abundance of everything in the shortest time possible. This is using the power of the universe to assist everyone to achieve their dreams.

The Vital Importance of the Brain

The mind controls the body in every possible way. So, starting with the power of positive thinking, this can improve physical and emotional health problems in providing increased energy. It also creates a more peaceful, happier, and calmer environment.

It is ale important in boosting our immune system, as well as how we react to viruses, bacteria and other pathogens which provides a more positive, optimistic outlook on life, which is ultimately better for our overall health and longevity. This in turn helps is with life situations and assists us to cope with challenges and see them as opportunities, which ultimately improves our wellbeing benefits.

So physical, mental, emotional, and spiritual health are all irrevocably entwined and as they combine to make us feel unwell, so they can also combine to make us feel better.

The Brain

The objective left side of the brain is considered to be adept at tasks that involve logic, such as language and analytical thinking. This includes numbers as well as reasoning and creating objectives. The subjective right side of the brain is best at expressive and creative tasks such as reading emotions, recognising faces and music. From this objective, it assists in understanding your strengths and weaknesses within certain areas that can help you to develop better ways to study and learn. For example, anyone who has a difficult time in following instructions can benefit by writing down the directions and developing better organisational skills.

Creativity

Creativity is the capability or act of conceiving new and imaginative ideas which are characterised by the ability to perceive the world in new ways and to find hidden patterns to make connections between seemingly unrelated phenomena and to generate solutions. There are many different ways of stimulating the brain to be more creative. One way to achieve this is called going down to level. This means that we are connecting to the right side of the brain to enhance its capability of expressive and creative ideas. These can then be used to work out a plan of integration for problem solving.

Implementation

First of all, sit in a chair comfortably then close your eyes and raise them upwards at 45°. Then take three breaths of air and slowly breathe out.

Finally imagine that you are now in a pleasant place that you are happy with, i.e., sitting by the seaside, in a field of flowers or somewhere you feel totally comfortable and feeling well at ease. Then let your mind drift for a while wherever it wants to go while still feeling relaxed. Then try to connect with the problem that you have or think about being creative about your environment or ideas, give the brain time to expand on its creative capability, providing you with the possible solution or expanding into other thoughtful ideas.

It does take some time to get used to working with the brain in this unusual way, but the results can be rewarding if you want to be more creative in any way to enhance your success level within your environment in both personal and business opportunities. Also, when you have self-belief about your ability to create something or carry out a task, then your chance of success is improved exponentially.

But this kind of belief comes only with a positive sense of yourself. So, you need to think and believe that you are the right person with the right skill sets in the right place at the right time. There is no need to have any lack of confidence because you are more powerful than any issues that are making you feel small, so trust in yourself today.

Brain Problems Solved

Finally, let the brain work for you by solving the problem of trying to give up something that you no longer need in your life. The best example of this is trying to give up smoking. If you only give up one thing at a time, then the brain will keep reminding you that you still feel like having a cigarette. So instead of giving up one thing at a time, you need to give up three things at a time. This is because the brain will stop hinging on one thing and now has a much larger base of problems to think about. Hence it is much easier to give up smoking in this simple way. It does not matter which other two things you are going to give up, but it will enable you to not smoke in the future within a very short period of time.

Brain Stimulation

A) Mental stimulation

Brain activities stimulate new connections between nerve cells and assists in creating new cells within the brain. So, there are many ways to keep your brain staying healthy in helping to assist your memory, concentration and focus on daily tasks both quicker and easier to enable the brain to remain sharper as you get older.

B) Physical exercise

Using your muscles in exercising can assist your body to support the increase in the number of tiny blood vessels to bring oxygen rich blood to the region of the brain that is responsible for thought.

C) Cholesterol

High levels of LDL high cholesterol can increase the risk of dementia. So, the importance of diet, exercise, weight control and no tobacco will go a long way in improving your cholesterol levels, which also helps the brain to think properly.

D) Social networks

Strong social ties and communicating with people have been shown to lower the risk of dementia, enabling the brain to perform naturally.

E) Caffeine

Caffeine is a natural stimulant that can improve your brain function and make you feel more energised and alert.

F) Ginko Biloba

This popular ingredient has been used for centuries to treat various conditions. Among its benefits are increased blood flow to the brain, which is believed to help and improve cognition. i.e., improving knowledge in the widest sense that creates more sensation and perception. It also has the potential to help treat Alzheimer's disease.

G) St John's Wort

This includes chemicals that can help regulate the mood and improve focus of the mind.

H) Bacopa Monnier

Being a natural herb, it has been tested for improved effects on cognition and improves correlation with improved memory. It also alleviates anxiety and stress.

So, the brain is involved in everything that we do and just like any other part of the body, it needs to be cared for. Exercising the brain to improve memory, focus and daily functionality is a priority for most people.

Especially as we get older, the benefits of incorporating additional tasks can assist you in keeping your brain young and more effective as follows:

- Play cards, strategy games and puzzles.
- Build your vocabulary.
- Dance on your own or with a partner.
- Learn a new skill.
- Listen to all types of music.
- Meditate every day.
- Learn a new language.

Winston Churchill

Winston Churchill made planning and decision making both political and military as well as making it simpler and more efficient. The force of his personality was instrumental in agreeing with the big alliance countries, including Britain's powerful alliance with Russia and the US. He had unbounded energy and determination. In the early days of war, he had few real weapons, so he attacked with words instead. The speeches he gave were among the most powerful given in the English language. His words were defiant, heroic, and human, lightened by flashes of humour. They reached out to everyone in Britain and across occupied Europe and throughout the world. He certainly used words as weapons together with his force of personality being instrumental.

He adapted two grand goals to defeat the Germans and avoid unnecessary carnage. His grand strategy was to weaken Germany by attacking its more vulnerable periphery in operating up new fronts in distant theatres.

First, he made up a list of all the armament which the Germans had, including personnel. Then he would look at each individual sector to establish its strengths and weaknesses, analysing all of the details he knew about. Alongside this by comparison, he would list all of the UK capabilities to understand where our advantages were over the German army. This allowed him to strengthen the areas where the UK was weak and to improve them. He then attacked the strategic areas where Germany was weak.

So, once he had recognised and understood the weak areas within their military strategy, he would then advance and attack these specific targets. Again, when he understood and analysed the weaknesses of our battlefield plan, then he would make sure that these areas were safer and more powerful.

Strategy

Looking at this situation, you can mirror this strategy that is used here with your customers to increase your business level. So, make the same list of weaknesses and strengths for your customers and your company to see if there are any particular areas whereby you believe that they have weak areas that you can assist them with. Simultaneously look at areas where you think that you are weak in and work out how to reinforce them before you have a meeting with your customer. This should assist you to implement a battle plan in enabling you to understand you customer and your own company in developing more sales and improving your profit margin at the same time.

Churchill was a true British Statesman of amazing character, with many special qualities, including his tremendous ability to inspire people with his unique strategic insight. With his charming and effervescent personality, this made him an effective leader with an abundant amount of passion and emotional resilience that people admired. He was also a superb write with immense speaking skills together with a keen sense and interest in history.

Quotations – His Most Inspiring Quotes

"It is no use saying we are doing our best. You have to be successful in doing what is necessary."

"Success is not final, Failure is not fatal, it is the courage to continue that counts."

These dynamic Churchill quotes prove that he waw a powerful force in the twentieth century and beyond.

The Power of the Moon

The idea that the lunar cycle can influence people's behaviour dates back thousands of years. The word lunacy derives from the Latin *lunaticus* meaning moonstruck.

So, we all know that the moon controls the ebb and flow of the tides, but it also has other powers including the fertility of women, that can affect the menstrual cycle and that ovulation happens around the full moon, while a period arrives around the new moon. It is also believed that the moon is partly the energy of the universe which is linked to our inner world, our intuition and our dreams. As the human being is 60% water, it is obvious that it has further controls over our emotions and moods as well as different energy levels that affect us all. Humans are the only species that moves out of alignment with nature and the seasons. However, there are ways of using the gravity influence of the moon to enhance our lifestyle and to solve problems.

There are specific times when we can use the different moon cycles to good use that will enhance our capabilities and improve our lifestyles. Just as the moon pulls the tides, so the moon pulls our emotions and intuition to the surface, as it exposes all of the feelings that hide beneath our awareness. It can also help to show us where we need to make changes for the improvement in our lives. There are many different phases of the moon, covering many ways that it can enhance our most powerful achievements by living in tune with the moon.

Moon Phases

1) The dark moon begins ten days after the full moon and offers the chance to recharge your energies as this is the lowest energy point of the month. So, give yourself time to withdraw into yourself to take care of your own needs. Also, think of the moon as your own internal compass to guide you to where you are travelling.

2) The new moon is the start of the lunar cycle, this is when the sun, the moon and the earth are all aligned in the sky. The arrival of the new moon is like a breath of fresh air and life, once more, feels filled with new possibilities and opportunities. Giving you clarity on what you want in life.

3) The crescent moon starts three days after the new moon and gets brighter and bigger as a sliver in the sky appears, which has the intention of getting things done. As our energy levels increase with the waxing of the moon, this works alongside our motivation in achieving and doing things within our goals to achieve success.

4) The quarter moon starts seven days after the new moon and lasts about four days. As the moon grows bigger in the sky, she brings energy boosting inspiration and everything you need to make your

hopes come to fruition, so it is like the energy of the entire universe is on your side. So, be receptive to everything coming your way and hear every conversation. Keep your eyes peeled and be aware of new doors opening for you.

5) The waxing gibbous moon phase begins ten days after the new moon, and it holds all of the potential and power of you hopes and your dreams to come true. However, because of uncertainty, now is the time to write through the night, or dedicate all of your attention to finish a project. Perhaps it is easier to tune in deeply to what is happening in your life and see what is still left for you to do, as this phase brings the last big lunar push of energy to get things done.

6) The full moon arrives fourteen days after the new moon and appears full in the sky, having aligned with the sun. This is a peak energy time of the month, but it can also bring a lot of emotion as the moon draws our feelings to the surface. So, either you should be celebrating a goal that has been reached or seeing very clearly what has stopped you in the way of getting to reach your goal. You may feel frustration by a lost opportunity, but this moonlight indicates what you must be clear on and gives you the details on how to move forward so that tis setback does not happen again.

7) The waning gibbous moon phase begins three days after the full moon and indicates that this is the time to plan meetings. This phase helps you to understand all of the things that have stood in your way and why, providing a great insight into how you can change this

situation for the better. This is also the phase of communication to be seen and heard, as you still may need to get your message out there into the rest of the world.

8) The last quarter of the waning moon seven days after the full moon indicates letting go of problems. As the moon gets smaller, it shows that you need to make room for new beginnings and to let go of the old ones. This might feel as though things are changing, and you are at the crossroads in the cycle, but you may find that things finally start to come together. So, face up to these things and decide if you have to give up on certain goals. Hopefully, you can find a new approach that you can implement during the next lunar cycle.

9) Harness the power of the supermoon. A supermoon is when a full moon coincides with the moon closest to the earth and there are two supermoons each year. Their appearance is 14% bigger and 30% brighter. The supermoon will be on supercharge and is a perfect time to surrender and heal any emotional toxicity. To harness its powers, try writing down what you would like to feel, achieve, or leave behind and place this on a piece of paper either outside under the full moon overnight, or beside a window. Alternatively, you could try burying your piece of paper in the garden. Either way, your requirements should be provided in due course as requested, as the moon lifts your energy levels to the heavens, it enhances its power and then responds back to you in time.

Finally, there are apps available that track the moon's phases, such as apps.apple.com – moon calendar/phases

The Magic of Crystals

Quartz crystals have been on this earth since the beginnings of time and ancient civilisations have used crystals as protective talismans, peace offerings and jewellery. So, Quartz makes up 12% of the earth's crust and is used in almost every kind of technology, including timekeeping, electronics, information storage and in other ways. As crystals communicate through computer chips, this vibrational energy can be transformed into life giving elements, including healing and wellbeing associated with its connection to earth. When you wear these crystals close to the skin or place them within your environment then they pick up every thought, intention and your unique vibrational energy and then amplifies the positive vibes that you are cultivating.

It was Albert Einstein who said that everything in life is vibration and, just like sound waves, your thoughts match the vibrations of everything that manifests in your life. So therefore, crystals have healing powers that enhance the positive vibes of the stones and amplifies the thoughts within your mind.

Crystals are renowned for their healing and energising properties, but they also work in manifesting your intentions, including what you want to create in your life. All crystals are connected to the earth as they are tangible, physical forms that have powerful vibrations. This energy continues to connect with you when they are close to you or if you place them within your environment. With every thought and intention these crystals pick up on your unique vibrational energy and amplify the positive vibes that you re cultivating. This in turn can enhance your lifestyle and achievements in reaching your future goals which also assists in problem solving. As every crystal has a different high frequency of vibrations, this then transforms into your unique vibrational energy and amplifies the positive vibes that you are cultivating.

The following is a list of important crystals, each with different qualities and achievements that can assist you as a well thought intention is the starting point that instils into your daily thought patterns, which becomes part of its energy capability.

Conichalcite

A powerful crystal that encourages communication and free flowing energy, allowing you to make changes in your life where they are needed. It also gives you inner strength to make the toughest decisions which protects you from your worldly worries. This makes it easier to focus your mind and get into the zone which promotes intuition, independence, imagination and flexibility. It also helps to get rid of the baggage of past relationships and assists you in telling the real from that which is imagined in your mind.

It is advised to wash your hands after handling.

Clear Quartz Crystal

This crystal further amplifies your intentions by magnifying the vibrations of stones that surround it. This is because it will cleanse and re-energise crystals and has the ability to counteract negative energy blockages. To energise it, sit quietly with the stone in your hand and feel its white light fill your body with positive energy. Then contemplate your intention for the crystal to trust in the power of its vibrations which are harnessed from the earth.

Selenite

This quickly removes negative energy from the body and clears the aura around you by moving the selenite down the body from the top of your head to your feet. Repeat this cleansing ritual until you feel completely rejuvenated with positive vibrations. Afterwards, you will have restored a sense of balance and the protection of a white light that connects you to the universe. This will assist you to relax more and think about possible problems that you wish to resolve.

Amethyst

Well known for its powerful spiritual properties, it is an ideal crystal to place around the home as it is visually striking and acts as a wonderful meditation tool because it boosts your inner strength and provides spiritual protection. It will focus on your intentions wherever you are to emanate calming energies, inviting them in for you in abundance. This also works well as a complementary healing took both in yoga and meditation.

Citrine

This is a crystal that harnesses the power of the sun as it is infused with natural light as it restores and regenerates its powerful vibrations. It is considered to be one of the most powerful stones for manifestation, which helps to make your intention a reality. It also instils a positive outlook and stimulates the mind so that you are motivated to form good habits and are always filled with optimism.

Overall Achievements

Our thoughts create vibrations throughout the universe, which makes setting intentions a powerful tool for achieving happiness and wellbeing. So having a clear purpose in mind provides us with insight into our aspirations, dreams, and values. It also helps you to live in the present, instead of being caught in negative thought patterns. Intentions have the power to attract things that will make them come true. So, creating an intention starts by setting goals that align with your values, aspirations and purpose. Then you decide which areas of your life that need upgrading to find fulfilment in improving your relationships, career, social life, health, and community spirit by using the power of crystals.

Solving Problems Before
They Arise

Everyone in their lives will have problems to solve at some time or another. This may be small enough to handle or quite large and difficult to find the right solution. Some problems can be solved easily through experiences you have had in the past. Others, however, come from a distance or are too large to cope with without a proven formula that has proven to work in different cases.

For future problems, it is important that you step back and see the problem details in hand. This is achieved through broadened observation, using a more circular vision, which will assist in closing down some of the other visions which allows you to concentrate on the more important issues through a lens of opportunity. Further to this is to analyse the complexity of the situation and then select one major element to concentrate on, combined with how far away the problem is in conjunction with the timing involved.

So, this should further your awareness of the changing future of the problem that can possibly reduce the impact of the problem outlined before it reaches you. Do not be too concerned about any problem that you foresee in the future, as most problems either disappear completely or change in character.

Planning

There are easy steps to take in solving the most complex problems before they arrive. This method is based on clarity, focus, simplicity, and elegance. Following this process will be defining what the root of the problem is in terms of breaking it down to its core components, prioritising solutions and conducting your analysis, enabling you to sell the solution to other individuals.

So, start by working out a strategy of where you currently are now and calculate how you can prove and forecast what the future can bring. It is important to spend time in looking where you are at this particular instant. In addition, where are you going in the future. This includes proposals of planned changes in circumstances. Do not forget the importance of what has happened in the past, as you can learn from many occasions which did not go in your favour. Look and analyse the more important instances that happened and understand them in great detail, working out how you would solve the problem in today's environment. Quite often, looking at previous problems in detail can offer ideas and ways of solving problems currently now and on the future. So, analysing previous problems can easily solve future problems that you are familiar with in detail.

Important Points to Consider

1) Define the problem

Clearly study the issue of the problem in hand and analyse it from multiple perspectives. Check with your colleagues to see if they have any other ideas as different people can look at the same problem in many different ways.

2) Identify the issues

Break down the main component into smaller parts, such as cost issues, volume issues, price, and revenue issues. As you identify all of the possible issues then your chances of finding the main root cause will vastly improve. So, the structure overall will become more apparent, leading to you investigation and further analysis.

3) Prioritise each sector

Havin laid out all of the issues then you can start to work out each one separately to solve the solution. With a constructed list of hypotheses that could solve all of the issues and then you need to prioritise your efforts in working out how to prove or disprove every issue separately.

4) Analysis time

When you have identified the important solutions that prove your primary hypothesis is correct, then you have a valuable solution. Concentrating on a proven solution will allow you to be more efficient and getting the answers that you require more quickly which allows great efficiency.

5) Selling that recommendation

Now is the time to sell your recommendations to others so that it gets implemented. So, begin by transforming the hypothesis into a clearly worded solution, using the core analysis to prove your case so your recommendation is implemented for future success.

Planning

It is important to spend time in looking where you are at this particular instant and, in addition, where you are going in the future, which includes proposals of planned changes in circumstances. Do not forget the importance of what has happened in the past. You can learn from many occasions which did not go in your favour. Look and analyse the more important incidences that happened and understand them in great detail and work out how you would solve the problem in today's environment. Quite often, looking at previous problems in detail can offer ideas and ways of solving currently now and in the future. So, analysing previous problems can easily solve future problems that you are familiar with in detail.

Saving Time

Time is a precise commodity that is valuable to the individual as well as to companies. In fact, saving time is associated with saving money. If we can improve on time wasting habits, this will improve your concentration level, as well as building up your productivity. This method can save you up to 25% of your time available that can be put to better use in achieving the other, more important goals, that in the long run will improve your finances.

Key Points

1) Reduce the number of people involved in a meeting to the minimum (i.e., 4–6 maximum). This increases efficiency.
2) Reduce the number of tasks that you are involved in and only concentrate on the most important ones, which will allow you to move down the ladder to solve the remaining others later.
3) Do not allow other people to interrupt you when you are problem solving, as this diminishes your concentration, which loses you both time and energy in starting again from your task.

4) Do not clog up your mind with a bucket load of stuff or problems. So, cancel the unfinished items which are taking up more space within your mind. Then this allows you to concentrate on the more important tasks and gets you thinking further about the more important items to be solved.

5) Working with sounds around you can either improve your thinking process or create problems with your concentration. So, if you have a choice, choose something that soothes your mind and allows you to relax by putting yourself within an environment that calms you and enhances your focus and productivity.

6) Take a break on a regular basis, as this helps you to relax your mind about problems and items that are worrying you, even if you look out of the window, this allows you then to think more effectively. Also, thinking about your major tasks will enable you to work and think more efficiently, which assists you to bring in more creative ideas.

Importantly, saving time can provide you with a number of ideas to make you more money for yourself or increase the profit margin within you company or organisation. So, saving time provides you with more time to manage encompassing functions that you are interested in, which will enhance a more productive way of working. This also puts you under far less pressure to relax more and think about some of the more important things that you like doing, which will easily enhance your lifestyle.

Gaining Belief

Belief comes from an acceptance or habit of mind in which trust or confidence is placed in someone or something, even if it is true or not. It also gives you a feeling of being sure of someone or of something exists in addition to something else that cannot be defined in truth but is held as an opinion. This feeling provides the ability for yourself and other people to be confident in what they believe in. For example, when you have self-belief about yourself regarding your ability to carry out a task, then your chance of success is improved exponentially.

This kind of belief only comes with a positive sense of yourself. You then need to think that you are the right person with the right skillset in the right place at the right time.

Indeed, you do not have to doubt your abilities of what you can achieve, even if your confidence has taken a downward step. With self-belief this provides you with additional trust, faith and confidence that enables you to achieve anything that you want to accomplish in life.

So, belief is something that is accepted and considered to be true or held as an opinion. It is also a conviction of the truth in some statement, reality or some being or phenomenon, especially when this is based on examination of the evidence.

Also, feeling good about something that is right or valuable is a feeling of trust in the worth or ability of something, so belief is everything when you are looking out at your environment, but belief comes from within, and this enables you to achieve anything you desire.

So put your trust and belief in yourself, together within a state of habit of mind and you will succeed.

The Importance of Supplements

It is advisable to keep up to date within the marketing scenario. One of the best informative procedures is to read the supplements that come with the Times and other newspapers, where there are insertions at the weekend or with other issues. One of the best is Raconteur, which centres on important subjects for companies and individual information. Such subjects covered include:-

- Remote working.
- Business continuity.
- Digital transformation.

Each supplement goes into great detail about what is happening today with a good forecast for the future. It also keeps you up to date with new business ideas. All of these supplements are available from Raconteur, either online or by subscription, including back issues.

Other subjects:-

- Artificial Intelligence.
- Business continuity and growth.
- Business risk.
- Future of authentication.
- Connected business.
- Future of HR.
- IOT (Internet of things) for business.
- The future of advertising.
- Cloud for business.

(There are more than 56 back issues available at raconteur.net)

Sunday Times Rich List UK 147 Billionaires

Providing an outline of the companies, achievements, and financial data, which should be useful in flicking through to see if any of your ambitions and ideas can be achieved by using their principles.

UK Richest 1000 Companies

Information on how they have achieved their turnover and success.

UK Young Top 30 Rich List

Details of how they have achieved high growth opportunities within their business.

UK Mature Successful Individuals

They cannot give up running a business as they are still addicted to power and money.

Rich List

All of these companies and individuals have had major achievements within their own environment or working for major corporations. So, a vast amount of information can be gained by reading through their ideas and achievements and matching this against all of our wishes and dreams of setting up a company which succeeds in achievements of all of our ambitions in life.

The Sunday Times

Top track 100 Britain's biggest private companies.

These are listed by their latest sales figures, with the vast majority in good health, with 474 companies reporting a sales growth year on year of 8%, taking the total to £237 billion turnover. 34 of this year's companies are owned by private equity firms, as well as a further 34 companies owned by founders and entrepreneurs, including 26 companies being family owned. With the top company (Ineos) turning over £25,000 million to the hundredth company (Peelports Group) with a turnover of £760 million, this list of companies is well written and has informative information including growth factor details. So, this should be of interest to all individuals and companies who wish to follow what these companies have achieved. As it is well written and informative, then this could provide you with overall ideas to assist you in building a successful and profitable company for yourself. This report has been created in association with the Sunday Times and Fasttrack. They also provide further company reports, including:-

- Tech track.
- Profit track.
- International track.

(These reports are available at fasttrack.co.uk)

Raconteur – Future of Advertising

Advertising is being reimagined and consumers are challenging companies to achieve more. But if over personalisation is strangling the creative process, let us look at other ways of how brands plan their campaigns in a saturated market. London is and will continue to be the hub of the creative and economic wheel of the UK, Europe and for much of the world. This gives us a unique position to be able to influence public opinion, providing an incredibly compelling opportunity to shape destiny for both today and the future.

Subjects covered:-

- Personalisation in a consumer-controlled future.
- When brands use ads to address business woes.
- Campaigning for that universal truth.
- The campaign for creativity.
- How advertising is shaping the future.
- Ads Add authenticity and action.
- Why the billboard is back.

Raconteur – Cloud for Business

Cloud technology can transform your business for the better. It also helps to overcome data quality issues in becoming more data enabled, with the impact of cloud technologies on employee development, the workforce and overall business performance. This enables the data centre sphere to continue growing with the usage of public cloud opportunities.

Subjects covered:-

- Why Cloud is more vital than ever.
- How Cloud communications are connecting workers.
- What data centres are doing to the world water supply.
- Embracing the benefits of private Cloud.
- Multi-cloud to empower digital transformation.
- The Cloud's cost/performance balance.
- 5G performance.

Marketing Advantage Company Reports

The company annual report provides important information for shareholders and potential investors, as the prime audiences are interested in revenues, expenses, profits, capital, expenditure and cashflow details for the company. This should also include marketing details for the previous years and expectations for the future, together with strategies, market conditions, significant business events, new management, and company initiatives.

In addition, the report can also be used as a vehicle to underline the company's successes. i.e., a new contract as well as a new product release which covers a specific market area. This information assists everyone to understand how the company has performed overall in the past and also provides an extremely good view of the opportunities that are available in the future.

Target Audience for Annual Reports
Employees

Management has an opportunity to praise employee innovation, quality, teamwork and commitment, all of which are critical parts within overall business success. This should also relate to the company successes, such as a new contract/product or cost saving initiatives and the expansion of new applications which have an impact on its workforce in providing reinforcement to the employees of the success that they have achieved.

Customers

Initiatives should also be included that shows how improvements in manufacturing processes have reduced costs, created quality, and enhanced its services capability. Sometimes as customers are maybe thinking of reducing their numbers of suppliers, but they still need committed and capable suppliers that are going to be around in the long term. They also have a requirement for quality suppliers of both goods and services incorporating their corporate mission and core values. Finally, the annual report should also show the company's strength in financial management.

Suppliers

It is also important that management send an implicit message to suppliers about the company's expectations of outside vendors. So, a profile of a supplier that the company has found exemplary can serve two purposes.

First, it rewards the supplier for its work and serves to further cement the business relationship. It also helps other suppliers with a better understanding of the level of service that is desired, together with the rewards that can be achieved for both parties.

The Community

This is where your reputation is important in developing the company's public image. This is an invaluable tool in stating their involvement in community projects, charitable contributions, and programs as well as volunteer efforts in protecting the environment.

Finally

Everybody within the organisation should be provided with a copy of the company annual report, so that they can discuss their position within the company, as well as the future potential details with their families and friends. This communication level of information could easily provide the company with enquiries and discussions for the important growth of the company. It does not cost much to enable everyone within your business to have a greater understanding of where the company is and, more importantly, where it is going.

Marketing Programme

Marketing is the business of promoting and selling products and services, including technical and research developments, as well as advertising with the emphasis on creating leads for new business generation.

Marketing Strategy

1) Work out a strategy of keeping in touch with your customers by introducing new products and ideas via email, social media and a monthly newsletter which should prove to be effective as most people are inundated with email information which, in many cases, is of no interest to them at all.

2) First of all, create funds for an effective strategy based on the expansion and sales forecast supplied from you existing customers and new customers to be identified. Just by asking your existing customers what growth do they expect in the near future, as this may expose any new business requirements they may have.

Marketing Responsibilities

Pricing

1) Offer a discount structure which includes both old and new stock for a short time period.
2) Provide a special offer price, which includes all of your old stock at a bargain.
3) Include a credit policy that allows a customer to pay monthly amounts over one year.

Promotion

1) Place advertisements in local and national press, including local town directories.
2) Publicity is free of charge so contact the local and national press for insertions, including a useful story behind the product.
3) Sales promotion starts with contacting your existing customers to see if any of them can recommend anyone who may need your products or services.

Positioning

1) Creating market research covering market developments, new products, and innovation techniques.
2) Working with the channel to create a coherent strategy for business development.
3) Set up and monitor a distribution network with products which are synergistic to their own.

Product

1) Branding across your communication channels will provide guidelines for your content creation team.

2) Outline your services in terms of back-up and support for existing and future customers.

3) Highlight packaging services with overall customer choice, including overseas shipments.

Social Media Marketing

Social media is a form of internet marketing that involves creating and sharing content on social media networks in order to achieve your marketing and branding goals. This includes activities including posting text and image updates, videos, including paid social media advertising.

So, with billions of users spending time on social media platforms around the world, it is well worth investing time and the overheads involved in having an engaging presence with the following sites: Facebook, Instagram, LinkedIn, Twitter and Pinterest. Before you begin creating a social media campaign, first consider your business goals. The following are questions to ask when you are defining your social strategy:-

- What do you expect to achieve by using social media advertising?
- Who is your target audience?
- Where would your target audience be and how do they use social media?
- What message do you want to send to your audience?

Your business type should inform and drive your social media marketing strategy in the right direction.

Marketing Newsletter

Publishing a newsletter gives you the opportunity to increase awareness and understanding of your company and its products and services. Customers and prospects may have a limited perspective of what your company can offer if they only view your advertisements or receive promotional emails. Newsletter content builds a broader picture to encourage readers to find out more, including links to more detailed information on your website. This will provide you with a low cost of communication with good results for its value.

Key inclusions:-

- Major new orders.
- Recruitment requirements.
- Print and send to top 20 customers.
- New offers.
- Promotion.
- Contact for more information.
- Highlight a product or service.
- Place newsletter on your website.
- Send out once a month.

Video Marketing

This should be a necessity in today's market. As text-based content just cannot compete with the power of video, which has a huge draw for an audience. The vast majority of people believe that watching product videos make them feel more confident and helps them to guide their online purchasing decisions, which improves your conversion rate into a sale.

Marketing Meeting

Everyone can gain experience and hew ideas from all of the attendees at this meeting. So, everyone should be prepared to discuss how they achieved a specific order in detail, covering how they won this achievement over and above the competition. Also, innovations are important to discuss the perception and experiments from all individuals as this should trigger similar ideas or information that can be followed up with similar or new strategies that can stimulate further discussion from the whole group of people. Always welcome and include a financial person in your meeting as they have may contacts within the financial markets, including details about other companies and competition awareness. This can assist you in the future in developing new contacts and potential customers.

Marketing Programme
The Importance of Security

The National Decision Model

This national decision model is a risk assessment framework and decision-making process that is used by security services throughout the UK. It provides five different stages that anyone can easily follow when making a security type of decision.

This is a framework that is designed to make the decision process easier and more uniform.

This can be used by all officers, decision makers and assessors that are involved in the complete process as it is not only used for making the final decision, but also assessing and judging them. This then enhances the opportunity to improve future decisions but helps to create techniques and methods for many different situations.

Security Plan National Decision Model Stages

Stage 1: First gather information about the problem, then work out what you know, but also what you do not know. All of this information will be used throughout the rest of the process then once your decisions are being assessed. They will be judged after the event.

Stage 2: The determine the threat, its nature, and its extent so you can assess the situation and make the right decisions.

Establish: a) do you need to take the necessary action straight away or is this an on-going problem.

b) what is the most likely outcome and what would be the implications.

Are your security people the right individuals to deal with this problem and are you best equipped to help resolve the problem at hand.

Stage 3: Knowing what the problem is will determine what powers you have in order to combat the problem. Work out which powers will be needed and also will the required powers and policies need any additional or specialist support to be instigated and introduced.

Also search to make sure if there is any legislation that covers this process.

Stage 4: Armed with all of the information regarding the problem and any policies and other legislations that may exist, then draw up a list of options, using this opportunity to develop a contingency plan or a series of contingencies that can provide you with a back-up plan if things do not go exactly to plan.

Stage 5: Once you have determined the most appropriate action, then is the time to put this into place, start to perform the most desirable action and, if required, begin the process again to get the best result possible. Then review the process and determine whether or not you could have done things better and what you would do in the future if you were faced with a similar problem.

So, this decision model makes the decision-making process easier. It is not only used for making decisions, but for assessing and judging them. It can also be used to improve future decisions and to assist in creating techniques and many different methods within many situations.

Policy – Be Safe

Policy is a statement containing a contract and agreement between a company organisation and other individuals. Policies play an important role in outlining an organisation's approach to various agreements to achieve.

Business policy defines your mission from within, which allows you to take decisions that employees will comply with. It also assists your customers in understanding your company rules and regulations. This ties down individuals in excepting the outline definitions and proposals as well as understanding the company's statement and regulations. So, policies are therefore the framework and constraints within the organisation which everyone can strive to achieve for both individual and collective success.

Too many businesses neglect to get even the basic policies written down early enough. So, there is a tendency to believe that their company does not need them and that spoken instructions will suffice.

How wrong can they be? By putting company policies down in writing makes them official. This then allows the employees to know what the company takes seriously and how they can keep up to date with their rights and responsibilities. People work better and are more satisfied when they know where they stand in any situation. So having ground rules established in the clearest and simplest terms is vital to limit the possible damage if a dispute happens. Therefore, written policies can be essential in ensuring a swift and fair outcome for both parties.

Equal Opportunities

Being an equal opportunity employer prohibits any company from discriminating against employees or job applicants on the basis of protected characteristic. However, this can also help your business for two reasons. First, it expands the pool of people from which to choose the best applicant for any job and secondly, it creates a fair opportunity for employees to co-exist, work, and thrive within this environment.

Employment Code of Conduct

All employers have expectations from their employees and a code of conduct can make this clear. Even if an employee has the best intentions and some things are simple enough to be understood, misunderstandings still may occur. One way to get over this is to have a written code of conduct that will include important elements like attendance and the use of social media.

Leave of Absence

For various reasons, ranging from health issues to vacation plans, employees may occasionally require to be absent from work. So, it is always advantageous to let your employees know beforehand what benefits you offer. There are different kinds of leave (i.e., sick leave, paid time off, maternity leave, and parental leave), however these are separate entities and may require different treatment in having all of this in writing alongside rules that are necessary to regulate with taking leave as the only way to adequately inform employees.

Employee Disciplinary Action

Occasionally problems will arise at work and dealing with them is easier with a clear disciplinary policy in place. Employees should know how and what circumstances they will be disciplined for. If you take a standardised, step by step procedure, then this will ensure fair an appropriate treatment. This will show that you are an employer who does not tolerate violations but also values remedial actions.

Finally, it is advisable to take extra care in consulting a lawyer to ensure that the procedures you have in place are lawful.

5G Opportunities

The main advantages with the 5G network are a greater speed in the transmissions, a lower latency and therefore greater capacity of remote executions. In addition, it provides a greater number of connected devices and the possibility of implementing virtual networks, called network slicing, for more adjusted connectivity in meeting your requirements, together with an improved network reliability.

5G has the potential to impact almost every sector but is particularly important to industries where data is a critical resource. So, the ability to transfer massive amounts of data with such low latency will enable ultra-immersive augmented reality providing gamin experiences. A 5G network can support more than two million connected sensors, which enables all sorts of sectors from smart homes to robotics to autonomous vehicles.

Automotive

Developments within the automotive industry could be a spur to improving connectivity, as cities become connected with sensors and cameras, monitoring everything from water pipes to traffic lights, with the increase of smarter cars will be able to tap into all of these systems, providing live feedback.

This will lead to making decisions on the fly which leads to safer and more efficient journeys.

Main Benefits of 5G

1) Reliability

5G is expected to be ultra-reliable, with no dropped calls or connectivity problems, which allows more critical use cases such as related to digital health and critical services.

2) Greater capacity

With greater capacity, it will mean that the networks can cope with many high demand applications all at once, providing virtual reality and simultaneous HD video streaming.

3) Flexibility

Network slicing allows a physical network to be divided into multiple virtual networks. So, this allows the operator to use the right slice, depending on the requirements of the user, providing data and alarm systems as a separate entity.

4) Improved battery life

Unbelievable, but 5G is expected to extend battery life of devices by up to ten times.

Benefits to Business Users

5) Business growth

It is expected that business levels will grow by up to £93 trillion in revenue by 2035, supporting goods and service in industries including retail, healthcare, education, transportation, entertainment, and many other industrial aspects.

6) Productivity

A major benefit is helping businesses to work more quickly and more efficiently in providing a saving in costs and therefore increasing revenue.

7) Flexible office spaces

These are smart buildings that will employ radio sensors to monitor occupancy, lighting, temperature, and CCTV coverage that will be streamed live to mobile devices. This will provide flexibility, efficiency, and security, ultimately lowering costs for workspaces, including for small and large offices as required.

Manufacturing

Companies around the world are facing pressures to deliver products faster and more cheaply. In addition to this, more products are becoming vastly complex. Therefore, there is a need to create smart factories that will make processes more efficient and reduce costs. This will then bring in further benefits of opening up other opportunities for replicating digital twins and remote maintenance.

Conclusion

So 5G networking will reshape business as the fifth generation of cellular wireless communication brings a revolution in the information age through enhanced internet connectivity. This will also benefit both large and small businesses, including markets in providing everything that is connected, processed, and digitised into a universal solution, with greater capacity of remote execution. In addition, it is also set to transform and advance many existing industries on a global basis for future generations.

IOT – Internet of Things

Understanding IOT

IOT is with us today in many different applications, assisting with our lifestyle requirements. As more innovations change and improve in the future, this will provide a living and breathing template that will balance our needs for improvements for a very long time to come. So, look at IOT as an opportunity in resolving problems of today and a long term solution for the future. It also promises a cast new world in connectivity and speed for data transmission and new applications.

IOT Innovations

1) Modular farms

Modular farms have been reimagined by operating them as vertical farms, where produce grows at different levels, built into containers which perform high efficiency and performance. This requires far less labour with improved yields of up to ten times normal output. The benefit is that IOT devices in the container unit monitor the environmental factors such as temperature, humidity, control feeding and watering. This provides a high level of automatic functions that are not required by human intervention.

For example, if a device is working outside of its parameters, then a system will send out an alarm signal to your central station or iPhone if required. So, this will enable you to respond and rectify the problem concerned.

2) Home and business security

There is a mobile app available which can generate unique PIN codes, allowing people to access properties in real time without using a physical key. You can also create time-sensitive PIN codes providing start and end times to ensure the property is secured after each departure. Users can also unlock the smart mortise with a high security fingerprint id using a concealed biometric sensor. Owners can also access activity logs, which show dates and times of visitor access. This provides a high level of security for all individuals, together with peace of mind.

3) Intelligent gardens for smart homes and business

This is a personal smart garden for growing your own produce in providing both tasty fruit and vegetables at a much lower cost with no maintenance required. There is an app that provides advice on how to plant and maintain the plants. Watering is fully automated, and the application predicts the dose of water to be released according to the humidity levels and the needs of the plant. How wonderful – it is behaving like an invisible gardener, doing all the hard work while you are away.

4) Track anything, anywhere, any time

There is now available a small tracking device that operates through a 5G mobile network and also through a direct globalstar satellite network, so that belongings can be tracked even in the most remote locations. This device is water resistant and wearable or fits in your pocket for convenience. All sorts of belongings can be protected including laptops, briefcases, equipment, plus children and pets. If any item is moved or if it has gone into or out of a specified area, then an alarm will warn you of its movements. So, this enables you to feel secure over a 24 hour surveillance system working for you.

Smart Weather Reporting and Reporting Systems

Updating reports manually is time consuming, hence the requirement for automated reporting updates as they happen. This brings in a solution where the system monitors temperature, humidity, rain sensors and cloud movements by providing weather statistics online. It works constantly and sends data via a microcontroller to the web server using the Wi-Fi internet. This system allows the user to set a threshold for a particular situation and alerts the user if the weather reporting details crosses the threshold of the values set. This system does not need human attention to monitor anything, as it is a fully automated system in its behaviour. Using internet connection, at both ends, it can collect data within tough environments, including volcanoes, dangerous minefields, polar zones, and a situation leading to a possible disaster. This will assist in real time alerts for pending weather tsunamis.

Data Analytics for Business Efficiency

Businesses are increasingly using IOT data analytics to determine trends and patterns by analysing large and small amounts of data. There are data analytical apps that can analyse structured, unstructured, and semi structured data to extract meaningful insights. This can also be applied to investigate different types of data including motion data sets, geographical data, and healthcare data. It can, in addition, be used by businesses for predictive and descriptive analysis to improve customer knowledge, enhance operational efficiency and create overall business value. This in turn allows task automation and remote control of devices to maintain an optimised balance between energy usage and conservation.

Healthcare and Fitness

There are now many devices available that greatly simplify the control and monitoring requirement over the treatment or the wellbeing of the patient or the person that needs some form of assistance and support. IOT supplies the current status and progress of each individual in terms of blood pressure, pulse rate, heart rate and respiratory rate as things change. This simplifies the control over the treatment of the patient in knowing what the biometric parameters are in real time. With the use of bracelets or pads equipped with sensor that can transmit information to a doctor, physician, or fitness coach, this then makes them very efficient in responding to their changing needs as required. This has a great potential for all of the medical staff, A&E, as well as care home patients to receive an efficient response and care for their requirements.

So just imagine that the technology of tomorrow is with us today.

Vitamins – Providing Efficiency

Vitamins are organic substances necessary for life. They provide growth, vitality and general wellbeing in protecting our bodies from free radicals and oxidations that can cause damaged cells to weaken the immune system.

Just as they are important to everyone's lifestyle, vitamins are also complex molecules that regulate the body's chemical mechanisms. They also contribute to storing and releasing energy, as well as repairing cellular damage. This is hugely important to your body for the healing process to work, as well as regulating metabolism and helping to maintain the quality of our nerves.

Vital Vitamins

It is no longer questioned that optimal nutrition can pave the way to optimal wellbeing. With more people living longer and wanting to do so while staying youthful and healthy, this provides a guide to all of the nutritional pathways and vitamins available, including the benefits and advantages associated with vitamin supplements that have become a necessity in today's lifestyle.

So, vitamins are crucial in increasing your vitality and energy in assisting you in making more useful persona and business decisions.

Vitamin A

This vitamin is useful in building resistance to respiratory infections and providing proper function of the immune system, which can lead to shortening the duration of the disease.

Vitamin B Complex (B1, B2, B3, B5, B6, B12, B13, B15, B17, H, Choline, Folic acid, Inositol Paba)

- Improves your mental attitude.
- Promotes healthy skin, nails and hair.
- Increases circulation and reduces high blood pressure.
- Strengthens the immune system.
- Improves concentration, memory and balance.
- Reduces premature ageing.
- Speeds recovery from fatigue.
- Possible caner controlling and preventative properties.
- Aids in keeping hair from turning grey as well as preventative treatment for badness.
- Helps control cholesterol build-up and aids in the treatment of Alzheimer's disease.
- Reduces the risk of heart disease.

- Keeps skin healthy and smooth.
- Fights infection by building antibodies.

Vitamin C

- Heals wounds, burns and bleeding gums.
- Offers protection against many forms of cancer.
- Lowers incidences of blood clots in veins.

Vitamin D

- Helps to boost the immune system in reducing the effects of viruses.
- Assists in the treatment of conjunctivitis.

Vitamin E

- Supplies oxygen to the body to give you more endurance.
- Protects your lungs against air pollution.
- Helps prevent various forms of cancer.

Vitamin F

- Aids in preventing cholesterol deposits in the arteries.
- Combats heart disease.

Vitamin K

- Helps in preventing internal bleeding and haemorrhages.
- Assists to promote proper blood clotting.

Vitamin P

- Helps to build resistance to infection.
- Strengthens the walls of capillaries, thereby preventing bruising.

Vitamin T

- Assist in blood coagulation and the forming of platelets.
- Also wards off certain forms of anaemia and haemophilia.

Vitamins are absolutely essential to the body's performance and its wellbeing. Particularly as some vitamins are not created within the body, so you may have to either move to an improved diet or take supplements to achieve the required results that you are looking for.

Marvellous Minerals

Minerals are essential in maintaining your body and mind to stay healthy and function properly. Your body uses minerals for example in keeping your bones, muscles, heart, and brain in proper working order.

They are important for making enzymes, which are biological molecules that significantly speed up the rate of virtually all chemical reactions that take place within cells. They are vital for life and serve a wide range of important functions in the body, such as aiding in digestion and metabolism. Minerals are also important in making hormones, which are chemical messengers, travelling through your bloodstream to tissues and organs.

They assist growth and development, including how your body gets energy from the food you eat.

Important Minerals

1) Sodium/Chloride

Needed for proper fluid balance, nerve transmission and muscle contraction.

Sources: Table salt, Soy sauce, processed foods, small amounts in milk, breads, vegetables and unprocessed meats.

2) Potassium

Required for proper fluid balance, nerve transmission and muscle contraction.

Sources: Meats, milk, fresh fruits and vegetable, whole grains and legumes.

3) Calcium

Important for healthy bones and teeth and helps muscles relax and contract. Also assists in nerve functioning, blood clotting, blood pressure regulation and the immune system health.

Sources: Milk products, fish with bones, fortified soy milk, greens and legumes.

4) Phosphorous

Important for healthy bones and teeth. Found in every cell system that maintains the acid-base balance.

Sources: Meat, fish, poultry, eggs, milk and processed foods.

5) Magnesium

Found in bones, needed for making protein, muscle contraction, nerve transmission and immune system health.

Sources: Nuts and seeds, legumes, leafy green vegetables, Seafood, chocolate and artichokes.

6) Sulphur

Sourced from protein molecules. This has antibacterial effects against the bacterial that causes acne.

Sources: Mainly protein – meats, poultry, fish, eggs, milk, legumes and nuts.

7) Iron

Part of a molecule – haemoglobin found in red blood cells that carries oxygen in the body, which is needed for energy metabolism.

Sources: Meats, fish, poultry, eggs, dried fruits, leafy green vegetables and cereals.

8) Zinc

Part of many enzymes needed for making protein and genetic material. It has a function in taste perception, wound healing, production of sperm, including the immune system health.

Sources: Meats, fish, poultry, leavened whole grains and vegetables.

9) Iodine

Found in the thyroid hormone which helps to regulate growth, including both physical and mental development.

Sources: seafood, iodised salt, bread and dairy products.

10) Selenium

Antioxidant enzymes that protect the body against oxidative damage.

Sources: Meats, seafoods and grains.

11) Copper

Part of many enzymes needed for iron metabolism.

Sources: Legumes, nuts and seeds, whole grains and organic meat.

12) Manganese

Part of many enzymes. Helps bone formation and energy metabolism.

Sources: Widespread in foods, especially plant foods.

13) Fluoride

Involved in the formation of bones and teeth. Also helps to prevent tooth decay.

Sources: Fluoride water, fish and most teas.

14) Chromium

Works closely with insulin to regulate blood sugar-glucose levels.

Sources: unrefined food, liver, brewer's yeast, whole grains, nuts and cheese.

15) Molybdenum

Part of some enzymes. Helps to prevent toxins from building up in the body.

Sources: Breads and grains, leafy greens, vegetables, milk and liver. The main attributes for minerals are as follows:-

- Creates brain development and behaviour.
- Improves cognitive abilities.
- Provides the formation of bones and teeth.
- Maintains the balance in the body.

So, it becomes obvious that when you take the right quantity and levels of minerals as an intake for the body and brain, the benefit is that they assist in keeping everything that is important to the individual, such as performance and also assists lifestyle activities.